9   8   7   6   5   4   3   2   1
Digit on the right indicates the number of this printing

Library of Congress Control Number: 2008931723
ISBN 978-0-7624-3656-9

Conceived, compiled, and illustrated by Monica Sheehan.
Produced exclusively for
Running Press Book Publishers.

Running Press Book Publishers
2300 Chestnut Street
Philadelphia, PA 19103-4371

Visit us on the web!
www.runningpress.com

for my sister
mary jane

(our cheerleader for love)

There is no remedy
for love...

but to love more.

—THOREAU

The Book
of
LOVE

afraid to love.

LOVE at first sight.

BLIND
Love

looking

love.

for

finding

love!

Too **young** to love.

Ready for Love!

STORY

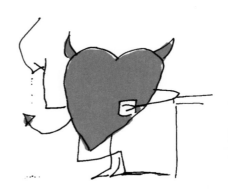

LOVE

ALLINLO

VEISFAIR

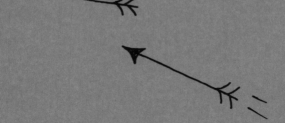

Unattainable

love.

COMPLICATED
LOVE

puppy love!

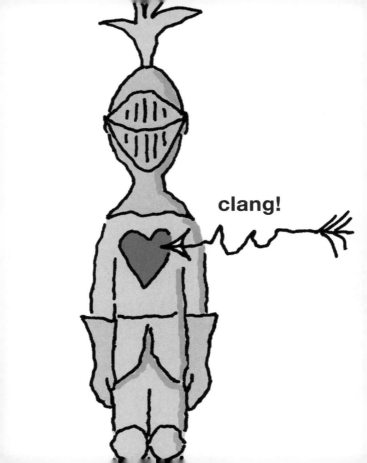

LoVe nest

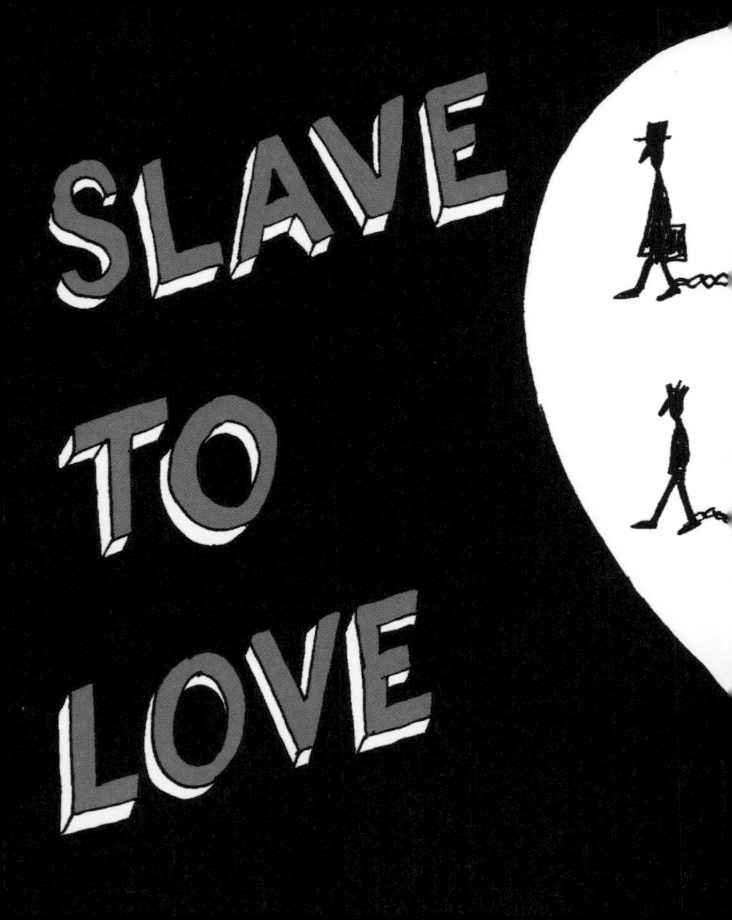
SLAVE
TO
LOVE

chas

ing after

(tired of love.)

lovesick.

The

Game

of

Love

L ♥

Love Letter

UNREQUITED
LOVE.

sweet love.

WAITING...

experienced:
in love

MAD
(about love.)

love birds

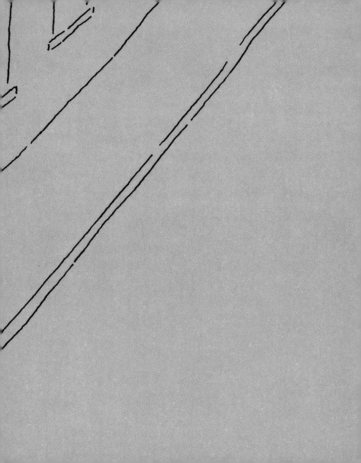

Love
for
Sale

when love

comes
knockin'.

Sea
of
Love

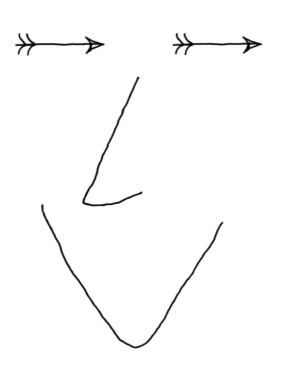

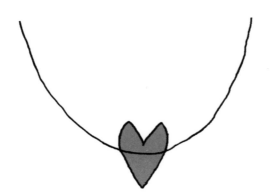

Addicted to *Love*

unlucky in love.

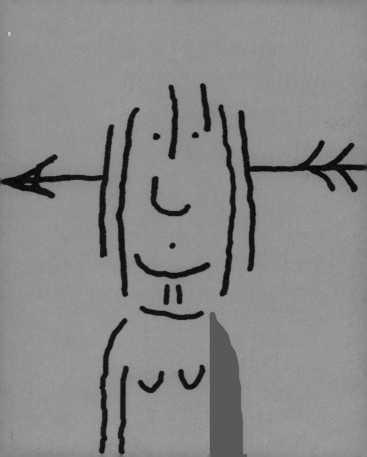

LOVE ON THE ROCKS.

conSume

by love

love

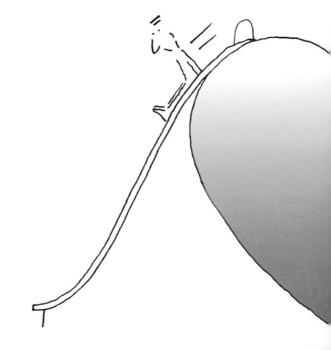

fades

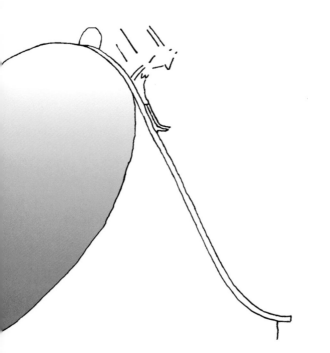

love hurts.

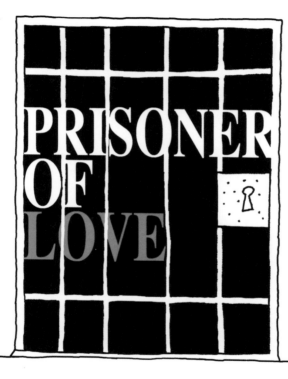

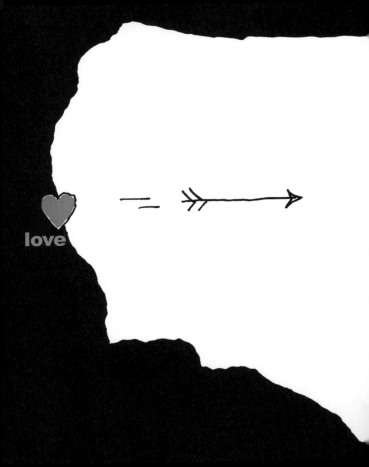

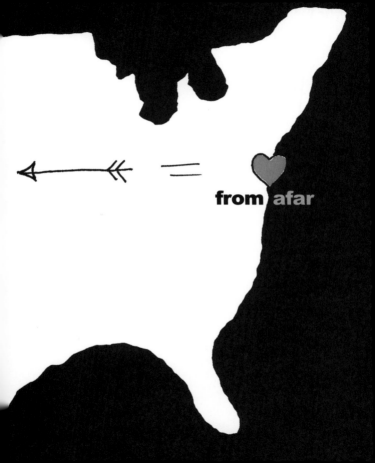

love

BLOOMS

CARELESS :

taking a char

long

lost

love

Love.

(Making)

LOVE

LOVE'EM AND LEAVE'EM.

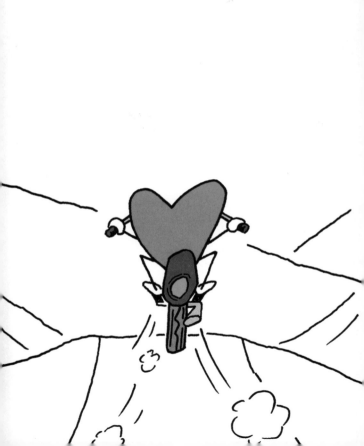

fools

in

love.

love endures

yeah!!

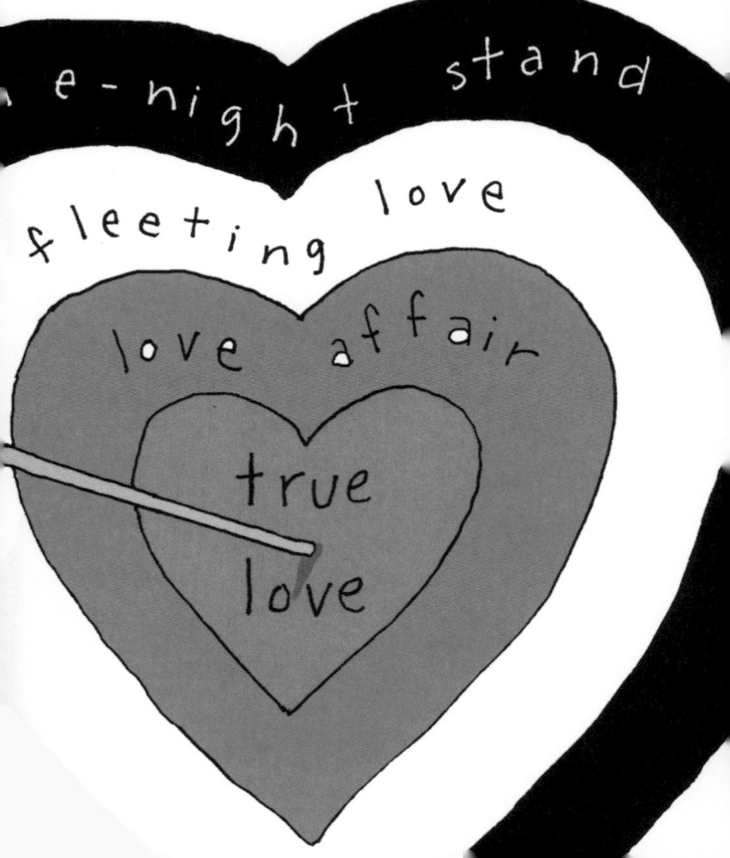
e-night stand
fleeting love
love affair
true love

LoVe...tHE SeCo

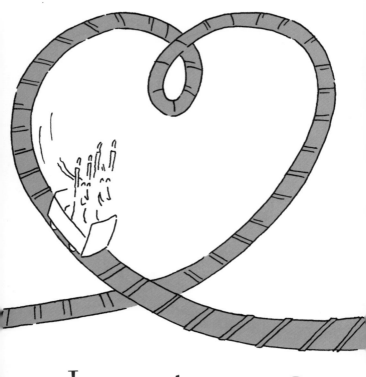

TIME AROUND.

$\mathscr{S}$wept *au*

(love is the answer.)

love is a man

plendored thing!

LOVE
CONQUERS ALL

all you need is love.

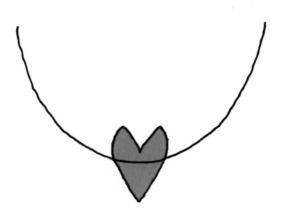